Families

Written by Daisy Baez

MODERN CURRICULUM PRESS

Program Reviewers

Becky Dugan, *Teacher*
Brady Elementary School
Little Rock, Arkansas

Judy Stobbe, *Bilingual Teacher*
Alianza School
Watsonville, California

Debra List, *Teacher*
Hansberry Child-Parent Center
Chicago, Illinois

Wanda Tansil, *Teacher*
University Terrace School
Baton Rouge, Louisiana

Executive Editor: Dorrie Berkowitz

Associate Editor: Marcia Formichelli

All photographs are by Silver Burdett Ginn (SBG) unless otherwise noted.

1: b.r. inset, ©Visual Horizons/FPG International.. 4. ©Richard Hutchings/Photo Researchers, Inc. 5: ©Frank Siteman/Tony Stone Images 6: ©Shahn Kermani/Gamma Liaison Network. 7: ©Robert C. Burke/Liaison International. 8: ©Shahn Kermani/Gamma Liaison, Inc. 9: ©Chip Henderson/Tony Stone Images. 10: ©Tom McCarthy Photos/Unicorn Stock Photos. 11: ©Elan Sun Star/Tony Stone Images. 12: ©Frank Siteman/Tony Stone Images. 13: Chuck Keeler/Tony Stone Images.

MODERN CURRICULUM PRESS
An imprint of Paramount Supplemental Education
250 James Street
Morristown, New Jersey 07960

Copyright © 1995 Modern Curriculum Press

ISBN: 0-8136-7991-5 (single copy)   0-8136-7992-3 (6-pack)

2 3 4 5 6 7 8 9 DP 99 98 97 96 95

You are part of a family.

Some families are big.

Other families are small.

Some families have many children.

Other families don't have any at all.

Some children look like each other.

Some look like their father or their mother.

Some families have many grown-ups.

Some only have one or two.

There are many kinds of families,
but one thing is true.

You are special to your family, and ...

your family is special to you.